ON HIGHLAND LINES

Robert Robotham

Right:
Forres was the junction between the
Highland Railway's original main line
to the south and the line eastwards
towards Keith. Here 'Black 5'
No 44978 is pictured at the station on
the east to south curve at the head of
the joint RCTS/SLS 'Scottish Railtour'
of 16 June 1962. Note the presence on
the left of a Type 2 (later Class 24), an
indication of the process of
modernisation that would see steam
eliminated and many lines in the
region closed. *Colour-Rail*

First published 2000
ISBN 0 7110 2714 5

© Ian Allan Publishing Ltd 2000

Published by Ian Allan Publishing

an imprint of Ian Allan Publishing Ltd, Terminal
House, Station Approach, Shepperton, Surrey
TW17 8AS; and printed by Ian Allan Printing
Ltd, Riverdene Business Park, Hersham, Surrey
KT12 4RG.

Code: 0005/2

Front cover:
Tomatin station is situated 101 miles from Perth but was closed in 1965. A siding was provided here for the local distillery and there was also a loop. Highland Railway 'Jones Goods' No 103 is seen at the station on 15 June 1960. What a magnificent locomotive this is and it is reassuring to know that it is now preserved in Glasgow Transport Museum. *Derek Penney*

Back cover:
Heading north on the Highland main line, Pitlochry, 28 miles from Perth, serves one of the most important towns along the route. No D5382 is seen heading a Glasgow-Inverness train on 14 August 1965. At this date, the station was still served by an extensive goods yard. Today, Pitlochry still has a passing loop and substantial buildings. *L. E. Elsey/Colour-Rail*

Highland Locomotives in LMS Days

Below:
During the preparation of this book, some transparencies of original Highland locomotives still in service were discovered, albeit in LMS livery. Unfortunately, only one was suitable for publication: Classified '4P' by the LMS, the magnificent 4-6-0 No 14767 *Clan Mackinnon*, originally Highland Railway No 55, is seen here standing at Aviemore in July 1946. These powerful locomotives were designed by Christopher Cumming, who was Locomotive Superintendent from 1915 to 1922. The growth of traffic on the Inverness-Perth main line warranted the new 'Clan' class — numbered 49 to 57 (with no No 50) — that consisted of eight locomotives. Four were delivered in 1919 with four more — including *Clan Mackinnon* — in 1921. They turned out to be the last Highland locomotives designed before the Grouping. *Clan Mackinnon* was the last survivor of the class, becoming BR No 54767 at Nationalisation and being withdrawn in 1950. *J. M. Jarvis/Colour-Rail (LM71)*

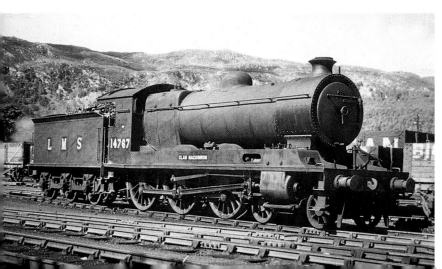

Introduction

This book looks at the lines of the former Highland Railway through a series of colour photographs taken mainly in the 1950s, 1960s and 1970s — a period during which there was significant change on Britain's railways. Indeed, this change is well illustrated from the variety of locomotives, rolling stock and liveries seen in this book.

The Highland Railway was originally conceived to transport agricultural products and fish from the region to the south. Mistakenly, it has often been assumed that it was built to carry goods and freight into the area, along with passengers, from the south, especially tourists from south of the border and rich landowners who had travelled up from London to their estates in the Highlands. But it was the Highlanders who built the Highland Railway and, to this end, it was like many railways, being sponsored by the local landowners of varying status and wealth. These individuals encouraged its building and expansion on their land. The lines also provided — and still do — a vital link through areas that are often cut off by road in bad weather. Not only were passenger services provided but also internal freight services over what may not be a vast network in terms of rail miles such as the Central Belt of Scotland, but in terms of geography is huge, stretching from Thurso to Perth (157 miles as the crow flies), and from Kyle of Lochalsh to Keith (110 miles).

The Highland Railway itself was a series of amalgamations of shorter lines that eventually formed a complete network. The line from Inverness to Nairn was opened on 5 November 1855. This was extended via Forres and Elgin to meet the Great North of Scotland line from Aberdeen at Keith, this latter line being known as the Inverness & Aberdeen Junction. The Great North of Scotland Railway had previously failed to reach Inverness from Aberdeen, so the new route was sponsored by two local landowners, the earls of Grant and Seafield. The relationship with the GNoSR was not always smooth, compounded by the fact that there were two stations at Aberdeen — at Guild Street and Waterloo — and transfers of passengers and mail were made by van or omnibus. This resulted in through traffic to the south being disrupted. Travellers were often stranded due to late connections and the whole arrangement was totally unsatisfactory. Seeking a more direct route to the south, a line was constructed from Forres to Dava and Grantown, passing over the Grampians at Druimuachdar — with a summit at 1,484ft — to reach Perth by linking with a line already constructed from Perth to Dunkeld & Birnam. The line was completed by September 1863. A nine-mile branch to Aberfeldy from Ballinluig was added by 3 July 1865. Running along the Tay Valley it was expensive to build, with 41 bridges and large earthworks. The direct link to Perth saved nearly three hours on the journey from Perth to Inverness compared with the route via Aberdeen. The line joined the Caledonian at Stanley Junction before Perth. Initially, there were disputes

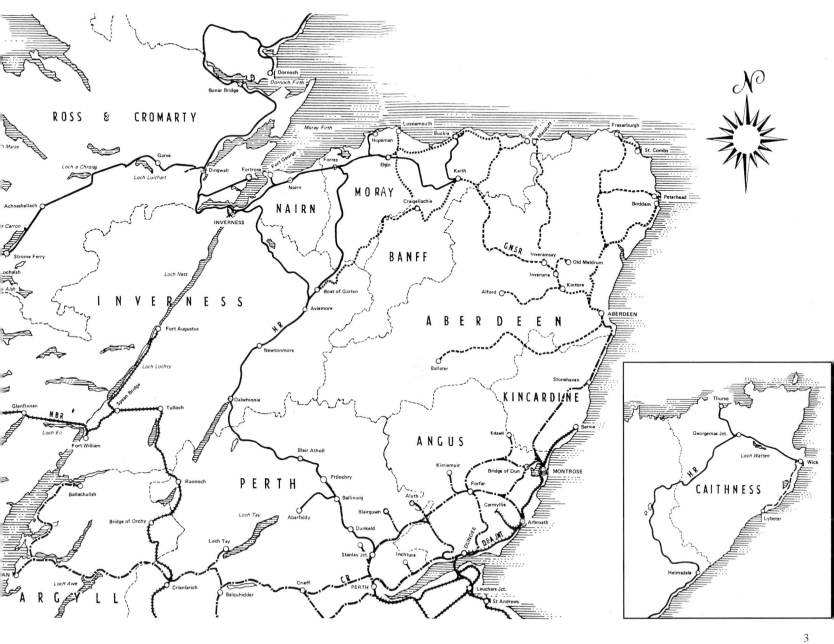

ROSS & CROMARTY

h Maree

Loch a Chroisg

Achnashellach

a Carron

Strome Ferry

ochalsh

Alsh

Garve

Loch Luichart

Dingwall

Fortrose

Fort George

Forres

Nairn

Bonar Bridge

Dornoch

Dornoch Firth

Moray Firth

INVERNESS

Loch Ness

Fort Augustus

Loch Lochty

NAIRN

MORAY

Hopeman

Lossiemouth

Buckie

Elgin

Craigellachie

Keith

Banff
Macduff

Fraserburgh

St. Combs

Peterhead

Boddam

BANFF

GNSR

Inveramsay

Inverurie

Old Meldrum

Alford

Kintore

ABERDEEN

Ballater

Stonehaven

KINCARDINE

Bervie

Edzell

Glenfinnan

NBR

Loch Eil

Fort William

Spean Bridge

Tulloch

Ballachulish

Bridge of Orchy

AN

Loch Awe

ARGYLL

Crianlarich

Balquhidder

Boat of Garten

Aviemore

HR

Newtonmore

Dalwhinnie

Blair Atholl

Rannoch

Pitlochry

PERTH

Aberfeldy

Loch Tay

Loch Tay

Crieff

Balliniuig

Blairgown

Dunkeld

Stanley Jct.

CR

PERTH

ANGUS

Kirriemuir

Alyth

Inchture

Forfar

Bridge of Dun

MONTROSE

Carmyllie

DUNDEE D&A JNT

Arbroath

Leuchars Jct.

St Andrews

N

CAITHNESS

Thurso

Georgemas Jct.

Loch Watten

Wick

HR

Helmsdale

Lybster

3

over running charges, which prompted the Inverness & Perth to consider an independent route. However, these were solved and following this, amalgamations of the Inverness & Nairn and the Inverness & Aberdeen Junction, in 1861, and of the Inverness & Perth Junction and the Perth & Dunkeld in 1864 took place. These two enlarged railways then amalgamated on 29 June 1865 to form the Highland Railway.

Turning to the north, a line from Inverness was authorised to Dingwall and opened on 11 June 1862. This line crossed an impressive viaduct over the River Ness, a swing bridge over the Caledonian Canal and a viaduct over the River Conon. The line advanced north to Invergordon, opening on 25 March 1863, and thence to Bonar Bridge on 1 October 1865. From here the Sutherland Railway was authorised to Brora via Lairg. This line was backed by a financial contribution from the Highland Railway, but the construction was so expensive that the line only reached as far as Golspie from where a road service was introduced for Wick and Thurso. The line was finally extended, due to the intervention of the Duke of Sutherland, as far as Helmsdale. This line was opened on 1 November 1870 as far as a temporary terminus at West Helmsdale. The Duke constructed his own station at Dunrobin, where trains called on request. He even had his own locomotive, called *Dunrobin*, and coach, the former of which now resides in North America.

The two most northerly towns, Wick and Thurso, had previously considered a railway to link themselves and, by 1866, the Caithness Railway was formed to do this, but funds were not forthcoming. The scheme eventually was realised by an extension north from Helmsdale — sponsored by the Highland Railway and the Duke of Sutherland — which joined the Wick-Thurso line at Georgemas, opening on 28 July 1874. Further to the south, the line to Kyle of Lochalsh was built primarily to open up the local areas and provide a link to Skye and Lewis. The Dingwall & Skye Railway reached Kyle in 1897. However, this was not until after quarrels that saw the line overcome the objections of the residents of Strathpeffer by a deviation from the planned route and a period when the line terminated at Strome Ferry, from 1870, with Kyle and Skye being accessed by steamer. The line was absorbed into the Highland 10 years later and the railway operated the steamer services until David MacBrayne took over.

Strathpeffer — a spa — ultimately did get a railway, from Fodderty Junction, which opened in 1885. Attention then turned to a quicker and shorter route to the south from Inverness. This new line was constructed from Aviemore through Carr Bridge, Slochd and Culloden, opening on 1 November 1898. Branches to Buckie and Portessie — primarily to access the fishing trade — were added prior to this on 1 August 1884. The Burghead branch was extended to Hopeman on 10 October 1892 and a line to Fochabers from Orbliston Junction opened on 16 October 1893. The Black Isle branch, from Muir of Ord to Fortrose, opened on 1 February 1894. More branches followed, the first being to Fort George from Gollanfield Junction, opening on 1 July 1899, and the last two branches opened being the light

railways from The Mound to Dornoch, which opened on 2 June 1902, and the line from Wick to Lybster on 1 July 1903. Thus, the Highland Railway was completed — a network that extended to some 506 miles and 31 chains.

Most Highland Railway passenger trains were austere compared with those of other railways in Scotland and England. Early stock was wooden-seated and it took nearly until the Grouping for vestibuled corridor stock to be introduced. Unlike some of the other railways, which had introduced catering on the train, the Highland had stops at certain stations for refreshments. Passenger services in general were aimed at a local service around Inverness, a local service from Perth to Blair Atholl and local services from Forres to Aviemore once main line services had been diverted through Carr Bridge. There was still a service to Aberdeen, and this was run in the main as a long-distance pseudo-express service and the main expresses to the south ran via Aviemore. The other service that connected with the Highland was the GNoSR line from Craigellachie and Keith that joined at Boat of Garten.

Freight business was extensive with fish traffic, coal and general merchandise — including oil and petrol from the south — and there was also a significant amount of livestock moved over the whole system. Many trains were mixed to economise, but freight traffic was particularly heavy on the main line from Perth to Inverness. The number of military bases on the network also saw considerable traffic develop. Postal traffic was always significant business over the Highland lines and there were TPOs to Wick and Inverness running well into the 1960s in service trains and considerable amounts of mail and parcels carried at other times on normal service trains.

On 1 January 1923 the Highland Railway became part of the London Midland & Scottish Railway (LMS). The LMS era saw an increase in the number of modern corridor trains with catering facilities. But, whilst the main lines did well, withdrawal of passenger services started on some of the branches — notably the lines to Burghead, Hopeman and Fochabers. The pattern of services remained generally the same with Sunday services being restored in 1929. Reductions in journey times were seen, especially with a number of named trains. The 'Further North Express' ran on summer Fridays only but by the summer of 1934 it was renamed the 'John O'Groat' and the following year ran every day. Also in 1934 two trains to Kyle, where they connected with steamers, were called the 'Hebridean' and the 'Lewisman'. In 1936 the morning Inverness-Thurso service was named the 'Orcadian' and connected with a ship for Orkney. The most famous name was the 'Royal Highlander' — the night sleeper service which had 3rd class accommodation from 1928 and which ran to and from King's Cross. By 1932 the Glasgow sleeper also took 3rd class passengers.

World War 2 saw only military traffic on the Fort George branch and the Lybster line closed entirely on 1 April 1944. Road competition continued to increase in the years following World War 2. This affected virtually all of the branch lines and it is a minor miracle that some of the main lines survived the desire to prune further — especially north of Inverness and the Kyle line. The first casualty of this period was the line from Gollanfield Junction to Fort

George, which had closed to passengers on 5 October 1943 and then ceased to carry goods from 11 August 1958 before official closure on 28 December 1961. The Strathpeffer-Fodderty Junction line was next, passenger services going on 23 February 1946 and goods services being officially withdrawn on 12 August 1951. The service from Muir of Ord to Fortrose — the Black Isle branch — lost its passenger service on 1 October 1951, with goods traffic lasting until 13 June 1960. The branch from The Mound to Dornoch was closed to both passengers and freight on 13 June 1960. At this time — again on 13 June 1960 — the local passenger service was withdrawn on the line north of Inverness as far as Tain and replaced by buses, although Rogart later reopened in March 1961. This mass closure had been preceded by only two other station closures, firstly at Mosstowie (between Elgin and Forres) on 7 March 1955 and Guay (between Stanley and Ballinluig) on 3 August 1959. The old main line, from Aviemore to Forres via Boat of Garten, was closed to passengers on 18 October 1965 with freight going in two stages: Dallas Dhu Siding-Forres officially closed on 30 June 1967 and Aviemore-Boat of Garten went on 16 June 1969. At the Perth end, Stanley Junction station closed on 11 June 1956 and the junction was remodelled with a new 1960s signalbox. By 3 September 1967 a further change was made when the ex-Caledonian Perth-Forfar line was reduced to single track and made freight-only when passenger services between Stanley and Kinnaber Junction were withdrawn.

In general, the post-Nationalisation scene saw the replacement of the remaining 29 Highland Railway locomotives with more modern power. The last two were Drummond passenger tanks, Nos 55051 and 55053, which worked the branch from Dornoch to The Mound. Replacements came with the introduction of displaced Caledonian types and the famous 'Black 5s'.

But, like other lines in Scotland, the diesels were to make an early impact — from as early as 1958. The actual train service pattern remained similar to LMS days, except for the withdrawal of many local services and a number of significant singlings of double track. The only new railway constructed during this period was the rerouting of two miles of the Kyle line as a result of a hydro-electric power scheme. But, in general, prospects for the Highland lines in the late 1960s and 1970s looked bleak. Beeching proposed that all lines should be closed north of Aviemore — an absurd proposition — but the oil boom came as something of a saviour, as well as the political unacceptability of cutting off large areas of Scotland and the Islands from railway lines that connected with the steamers. Oil traffic saw loops reinstated, double track sections restored and colour light signalling installed. Freight traffic boomed with the building of the oil fields, especially with oil pipes being fabricated at Invergordon, although general merchandise freight has always been difficult to sustain for any length of certainty and there have been disappointments, such as the closure of the British Aluminium smelter at Invergordon.

Road improvements to the A9 and other roads to the north and Kyle could potentially have hit rail hard. This is particularly true of the new road bridge at Dornoch but, despite this, most of the ex-Highland network lives on. This is despite radical closure proposals. It was proposed, for example, that the Kyle line was to close, only to be reprieved. Class 37s took over most services from the Type 2s in the 1980s and freight traffic, after the North Sea oil boom all but finished with the demise of Speedlink. However, Transrail and later EWS have revived services and Inverness even sees a Class 66-hauled container train from Mossend on part of the Harbour branch. There has also been a significant revival of timber traffic and growth in passenger numbers with new 'Sprinter' type DMUs now on most services. Some thirty years on from Beeching, the folly of the Report is again being realised as the remaining Highland Lines are still going strong today and Inverness has retained its Sleeper and a through day service to and from London. With tourism and leisure growing and environmental pressure and willingness to carry more freight by rail, the future looks bright.

Inevitably in a colour album such as this, space for text is limited and so the following books and publications can also be recommended to give the reader a more in-depth background to the Highland Railway.

Highland Railway Album; Anthony Lambert; Ian Allan
The Highland Railway; O. S. Nock; Ian Allan
Trains Illustrated: 'British Railways Then & Now, No 18'; Ian Allan
The Highland Railway; H. A. Vallance; David & Charles
Forgotten Railways: Scotland; John Thomas; David & Charles

In addition, much of the Highland Railway is still open to passengers and can be travelled on — indeed, this still has to be the best way to compare most of the photographs in this book with what the scene is like today. Also, the preserved line from Aviemore has also taken great strides recently and now operates into the original junction station at Aviemore on the Perth to Inverness main line before running to Boat of Garten and then with future extensions to come to Broomhill and Grantown-on-Spey. Well worth a visit and you can get there by train!

In putting this book together, I am especially grateful to Ron White, for all his help, Roy Hamilton, Derek Penney, David Cross, Colin Stewart for local input, and Jake Robotham who provided me with the inspiration.

Robert Robotham
Sherborne
March 2000

Perth-Inverness

Below:
Although Stirling is often portrayed as the 'Gateway to the Highlands', it was Perth that represented the effective southern terminus of the Highland Railway. There were proposals for an independent Highland Railway route into Perth, but these were never fulfilled and for the duration of its independent existence the HR was reliant upon the Caledonian route from Perth to Stanley Junction. Here 'Black 5' No 44701 awaits departure from Perth with a southbound parcels' train. *Derek Cross*

Below:
Pickersgill Caledonian '72' class — LMS-classified '3P' — 4-4-0s Nos 54485 and 54486 stand at Perth with the 6.5pm service to Inverness in May 1960. The train was specially organised for the TV programme *Railway Roundabout*. These locomotives were introduced in 1920. No 54485 carries a Perth shed plate and No 54486 is a Forfar locomotive. Perth station was opened in 1848 and designed by Sir William Tite. It was originally planned as a terminus and was ultimately the station at which North British, Highland and Caledonian railways all met. At Perth, Highland trains were often joined from two portions from Glasgow and Edinburgh to make up the main train. Modernisation in Scotland saw Perth converted from semaphore to colour light signalling by the early 1960s and there was also a new marshalling yard — built under the BR Modernisation Plan — although this is now reduced and used by the Infrastructure Maintenance Engineer. *Colour-Rail*

'Black 5' No 44720 heads an up express near Stanley Junction in August 1963. Stanley Junction was seven miles north of Perth and from here the Highland main line branched off from the now closed Caledonian line to Forfar and Aberdeen. The station closed on 11 June 1956, following which the layout was changed, with a new signalbox being added in the 1960s. The layout was simplified even further when the Caledonian line was closed to passenger services and retained as a single-track goods only line. It is plain line today following the closure of the remaining section of the ex-CR line in the early 1980s. Today, only the Highland route survives and Stanley Junction marks the start of the double-track section to Perth.
The Late D. M. C. Hepburne-Scott/Colour-Rail

Above:
The first station after Perth on the Highland proper was Murthly, 10 miles from Perth, which was closed on 3 May 1965. A DMU, forming a local to Blair Atholl, waits for the signalman to open the gates. The photograph is dated April 1965, only a month before the closure of the station and the withdrawal of the Blair Atholl-Perth locals. The footbridge at Murthly is original Highland Railway and there was also a small goods yard here. *George M. Staddon/Colour-Rail (DE1895)*

Below

Ballinluig was the fourth station on the HR main line and was a junction for the branch to Aberfeldy. The branch opened on 3 July 1865 and ran along the valley of the Tay. The two Type 2 (later Class 26) diesels, Nos D5344 and D5340, are in the early green livery that did not include yellow 'warning panels'. The BRCW Bo-Bos replaced the pairs of Class 5 steam locomotives and were to continue in this role for many years to come well into 'corporate blue' days. The branch closed to passengers in May 1965 only two months short of its centenary but, in July 1962, as the sign says, one could still 'Change here for Aberfeldy'. *C. Woodhead/Colour-Rail (DE1597)*

Right:

The Blair Atholl-Perth local service is seen again, this time at Ballinluig, with a DMU forming the 12.35pm train to Perth crossing a northbound service on 3 April 1965. By this date the Aberfeldy branch was living on borrowed time, evinced, perhaps, by the slightly careworn station nameboard. *Roy Hamilton*

THE LINE EXCEPT
BY THE
FOOTBRIDGE

BALLIN
JUNCTI
CHANGE HERE FOR

Far Right:
By April 1965, when the passenger service had one month to go, services on the Aberfeldy line were in the hands of diesels. Here, Type 2 (later Class 24) No D5122, built by British Railways, approaches Ballinluig, bringing its train — a single Gresley suburban brake composite — under the rather fine bi-directional Caledonian signal. *George M. Staddon/Colour-Rail (DE1783)*

Right:
Timetable in the Northerly direction for 15 June-6 September 1964. *Peter Waller Collection*

Below:
Caledonian Class 2P 0-4-4T No 55208, a representative of a type introduced from 1900, stands in the Aberfeldy branch platform at Ballinluig on 26 August 1959. These ex-Caledonian '2Ps' were used extensively on Scottish branch lines, often with the one coach that was sufficient for passenger traffic at that time. No 55208 was based at Perth. *George M. Staddon/Colour-Rail*

PERTH, ABERFELDY, BLAIR ATHOLL, AVIEMORE, FORRES, NAIRN and INVERNESS

Week Days

Stations (top portion): London (Euston) dep, Crewe, Edinburgh (Waverley), Glasgow (Buchanan St.), Perth, Murthly, Dunkeld and Birnam, Dalguise, Ballinluig, Balnaguard, Grandtully, Aberfeldy, Pitlochry A, Killiecrankie, Blair Atholl, Struan, Dalnaspidal, Dalwhinnie, Newtonmore, Kingussie, Kincraig, Aviemore, Boat of Garten, Broomhill, Grantown-on-Spey (West), Dava, Dunphail, Forres, Brodie, Nairn, Gollanfield, Dalcross, Allanfearn, Carr Bridge, Tomatin, Moy, Daviot, Culloden Moor, Inverness arr.

Week Days—continued / Sunday (See notice on page 2)

Notes

- A Pitlochry is the station for Kinloch Rannoch
- B Except Saturday nights but runs on Sundays. Dep London (Euston) 7 30 pm, Crewe 11 00 pm
- C Except Mondays
- C Stops to set down from Perth and South thereof on notice at Perth and to take up on notice at Dunkeld and Birnam
- D Diesel Service
- E or E Except Saturdays
- F Fridays nights
- g Dep London (Euston) 7 5 pm, Crewe 10 34 pm on Sunday nights
- h Sunday to Thursday nights
- O On Saturdays 20th June and 5th September 1964
- Q Arr Blair Atholl 7 9 am
- S Stops to set down on notice at Aviemore
- L Dep Crewe 2 18 am on Monday mornings
- M Mondays only
- MB Miniature Buffet Car
- P Stops to set down from England on notice at Perth
- S Stops on notice to set down
- RB Buffet Car
- RC Restaurant Car
- SC Sleeping Car
- s Saturday nights
- t Stops on notice to take up, also to set down on notice at Perth and to take up on notice being given at Aviemore
- TC Through Carriages
- T Stops on notice to take up or set down on notice at previous stopping station
- X Dep from Glasgow (Central) Station
- † Sundays only
- ‡ Second class only
- ✕ Except Saturdays and Sundays

For OTHER TRAINS between Boat of Garten and Grantown-on-Spey (East), see Table 41

Below:
Many of the trains on the Aberfeldy line were mixed and here Class 2P 0-4-4T No 55200 stands at the terminus at Aberfeldy with a train from Ballinluig in May 1959. No 55200 was a Forfar-based engine at this time. The Aberfeldy line was eight miles and 59 chains long and had two stations: a halt at Balnaguard and a station at Grandtully. There were no passing loops.
D. H. Beecroft/Colour-Rail (SC343)

Right:
Another view of Aberfeldy sees No D5122 with its train for Ballinluig in April 1965. Note the marvellous John Menzies bookstall on the platform. All services were withdrawn between Ballinluig and Aberfeldy from 3 May 1965, at which date Ballinluig was also closed. *George M. Staddon/Colour-Rail (DE1446)*

Left:
A rare view from the train sees two Type 2 Class 26 diesel-electrics crossing Killiecrankie Viaduct with a train for Perth on 9 September 1960. The train has just left Killiecrankie Tunnel and is crossing out onto the 10-arch viaduct. The Highland lines have some spectacular viaducts. These include the seven-span masonry structure over the Divie at Dunphail on the now closed section from Forres to Aviemore, which is 477ft long and 105ft high, a girder bridge across the Tay at Dalguise, which is 67ft high and 515ft long, and this 10-span viaduct at Killiecrankie, which is 54ft high, as well as the magnificent structure at Culloden. The station at Killiecrankie had a passing loop, although this was lifted in the 1960s. The station eventually closed to passengers with many others in 1965. *Colour-Rail*

Right:
Preserved 'Jones Goods' No 103 makes a fine sight as it nears Blair Atholl on 16 June 1960. No 103 was able to take part in the Highland Railway's centenary celebrations in 1965 before being retired to the Transport Museum in Glasgow. *D. Penney*

Above:
Caledonian '2P' 4-4-0 No 54486 rolls into the sidings at Blair Atholl, 35 miles from Perth, whilst working a pick-up goods service in May 1959. A bridge takes the line over the River Tilt into the station. The town of Blair Atholl is the location of the ancestral home of the Dukes of Atholl. The station had an extensive layout as well as yard and was also the start of the severe climb to Druimuachdar Summit. In addition, it possessed a locomotive shed, but this was closed in 1962 as the diesels took over and there was no longer a requirement to assist locomotives for the climb. Blair Atholl was the terminus of the local service from Perth that was withdrawn from 1965. *D. H. Beecroft/Colour-Rail*

Right:
Following the climb from Blair Atholl, Druimuachdar Summit — the highest railway summit in Great Britain — is then passed and on the descent comes Dalwhinnie. A Metro-Cammell-built DMU waits at Dalwhinnie with a return Strathspey Railway Association special from Boat of Garten to Edinburgh. During this period the line between Dalwhinnie and Blair Atholl was reduced to single track with Dalwhinnie being located 58 miles from Perth — halfway to Inverness. There was also a distillery here. *Roy Hamilton*

Left:
Descending through Glen Truin there was a loop at Inchlea as the line went on to Newtonmore where there was a one-time local service from Inverness. The preserved 'Jones Goods' No 103 is pictured heading the Highland Railway centenary special near Newtonmore on 21 August 1965. After an initial run from Perth to Inverness, the locomotive operated a number of additional specials between Inverness and Forres over the following week. *Derek Cross*

Right:
Three miles further on comes Kingussie where there is another loop and extensive buildings that housed a buffet on the Inverness side. There was a goods yard here, which closed in 1965, and there was also a distillery siding. On 30 June 1973 an up service from Inverness to Edinburgh arrives at the station behind two unidentified Type 2s, a Class 24 and a Class 26. *Colour-Rail*

Below:

After Kingussie came Kincraig, where there was another loop. This was lifted on closure in 1965 but then relaid in 1979. BR Type 2 (later Class 24) diesels Nos D5120 and D5124 stand in the loop here on 28 August 1965. At a distance of 35 years it is difficult to speculate on the topic of the crews' conversation. Perhaps they were lamenting the disappearance of the 'Black 5s' over the route?
K. M. Falconer/Colour-Rail

Right:

The next station northwards was the important junction at Aviemore. This was the junction between the original route to Inverness, via Dava and Forres, and the new line, via Culloden. The station also saw services to Keith via the GNoSR line to Craigellachie. This route left the Forres line at Boat of Garten. The station had many sidings with a locomotive shed (coded 60B). 'Black 5' No 45165 passes with a freight for Inverness on 15 June 1960. The shed was closed in 1962, but in 1950 Nos 45018, 54455, 54466, 54488, 54493, 55174 and 57586 were allocated, with Nos 42269, 45136, 54466, 54482, 54484, 54488, 55173, 57586, 57591, 57597, 57632 and 78052 in residence in 1959. *Derek Penney*

Left:
'Black 5' No 45470 gets away from Carr Bridge with a northbound freight for Inverness in 1951. There was another loop here and the signalman has lost no time in returning his starting signal to danger. *G. L. Wilson/Colour-Rail*

Below:
A 'Black 5', No 5014 in LMS livery, passes Slochd Summit signalbox with a down freight heading towards Inverness in August 1938. Slochd Summit is 1,315ft above sea level and was the location of a loop removed in 1963. The loop was subsequently to be reinstated. There was also a viaduct here over Wade's Military Road to Inverness and the railway, at this point, ran parallel to the main A9 trunk road. The descent from Slochd to Inverness is steep, reaching a gradient of 1 in 60 in places. *Colour-Rail (LM1)*

Above:
This is another photograph of No 103, but this time the 'Jones Goods' is accompanied by GNoSR No 49 *Gordon Highlander*. The locomotives are seen near Moy on 16 June 1962. This was another station that lost its loop on closure in 1965 only to have it rebuilt in 1979. No 49 was withdrawn from BR service in June 1958 as No 62277 and restored to its GNoSR livery as No 49, one of the quartet of locomotives representing the Scottish pre-Grouping railways. Unfortunately, at the time, no locomotives from the fifth company, the Glasgow & South Western, remained in main line operation. *Colour-Rail*

Right:
After Daviot came Culloden Viaduct. At 600yd in length, this viaduct is the largest structure on the Highland main line. Culloden Moor station came next on the descent towards Inverness and here two 'Black 5s', Nos 44785 and 44959, are seen on the slog up to Culloden with the 8.30am service from Inverness to Glasgow in August 1959. *Colour-Rail (SC848)*

Inverness

Inverness was accessed with the 'new' Culloden line passing over the original line to Nairn and Forres at Milburn. The station was accessed via Welsh's Bridge, and then some trains took the avoiding line and then backed into the Far North platforms at Rose Street. The station was rebuilt towards the end of the 1960s. Inverness — the Capital of the Highlands — was key to the English suppression of the Scots following the 1715 rebellion and was on the military road from Fort William to Fort George. There were a local services to Keith and Tain from here, and also an express service to Aberdeen that was converted to 'cross country' DMUs from 1960.

Below:
BRCW Type 2s (later Class 26) Nos D5322 and D5323 get away from Inverness with the up mail to the south — note the mail van behind the locomotives — on a lovely evening in June 1961. Inverness had a large goods yard and there was also a link to the harbour. Part of the latter is still in use today by English, Welsh & Scottish Railway services. *Colour-Rail (DE1709)*

Right:
A very smart 'Black 5', No 45472, leaves Inverness with a local for Forres in July 1957. The train is passing Welsh's Bridge where the lines to Forres and Culloden split. *T. J. Edgington/Colour-Rail*

31

Left:
Back in the station are two more Type 2s on the 11.10am to Perth, Glasgow and Edinburgh on 12 April 1965. The locomotives are D5325 and D5115 (later Nos 26025 and 24115 respectively). The train is in the Nairn line platforms at Inverness; the lines to the north had their own platforms to the rear right of this train.
Bruce Nathan/Colour-Rail

Below:
Inverness shed was coded 60A and had sub-sheds at Dingwall and Kyle of Lochalsh. The other Highland sheds were coded 60B for Aviemore, with a sub-shed at Boat of Garten, 60C for Helmsdale, Dornoch and Tain, 60D for Wick and Thurso and 60E at Forres. The ex-HR 'Jones Goods' is framed by the arch, which was actually the water tower, at the entrance to Inverness shed on 16 June 1962. It was originally intended that the locomotive depot would be a complete circle with the arched water tower as an entrance, but in reality it was never quite completed.
D. Trevor Rowe/Colour-Rail

Inverness Shed
— sample allocation (1959)

'Black 5' 4-6-0	44718, 44719, 44722, 44723, 44724, 44783, 44784, 44785, 44788, 44789, 44798, 44799, 44991, 44992, 45066, 45090, 45098, 45117, 45123, 45124, 45179, 45192, 45319, 45320, 45360, 45361, 45453, 45460, 45461, 45476, 45477, 45478, 45479
Class 3P 4-4-0	54463, 54487, 54493, 54496
Class 2P 0-4-4T	55198, 55199, 55216, 55226, 55227, 55236
Class 0F 0-4-0ST	56038
Class 3F 0-6-0T	56300, 56305, 56341
Class 3F 0-6-0	57575, 57594, 57661

Below:

A rare colour photograph inside the shed at Inverness, in 1958, sees Caledonian '439' class or Standard Passenger 0-4-4T locomotive No 55198, dating from 1900, on one of the roads coupled to what looks like the tender of a Drummond Caledonian 0-6-0 Standard Goods. The Caledonian locomotives were common on the Highland lines, lasting much longer than the original Highland locomotives. The shed roads were accessed by a turntable. The tenders of the ubiquitous 'Black 5s', representative of locomotives that dominated most of the passenger services before the introduction of the diesels, can be seen poking out. The shed closed in 1962 with the onset of mass dieselisation that started in the late 1950s. *Colour-Rail*

Right:

The Far North platforms at Inverness are seen on 15 April 1959 as a Caledonian '72' class 4-4-0 leaves with a local service for Tain. Sidings can be seen fanning out to the left of the locomotive as can the overall roof that covers part of the Nairn line platforms. These locals were withdrawn in June 1960 and replaced by buses. Many trains would reverse back into these platforms having come in from the south and vice versa when some trains from the north would gain access to the Nairn platforms. To the left are the old Lochgorm works, which were to become a diesel depot, and to their left was the avoiding line. Beyond this were Needlefield carriage depot and sidings. The avoiding line and the tracks from the North line platforms met at Rose Street Junction. *W. P. de Beer/Colour-Rail*

The Far North Lines

Left:
Heading west from Inverness on the Far North lines, the first station was located at Bunchrew, where 'Black 5' No 45479 is seen heading the lengthy 5.40pm service from Inverness to Kyle on 22 August 1959. This train would not be stopping at all the local stations between Inverness and Dingwall. *Colour-Rail*

Below:
Ex-Caledonian 0-6-0 No 57594 is seen at Muir of Ord station from the footplate of 'Jones Goods' No 103 on 20 May 1960. Muir of Ord was the junction for the Black Isle branch to Fortrose. This branch was closed to passengers on 1 October 1951 and to goods on 13 June 1960. The extra platform and yard can be seen to the right of the train. *Colour-Rail*

Below:
No 57594 is seen again, but this time on a railtour — the Stephenson Locomotive Society's 'Scottish Rambler' — at the terminus at Fortrose on 14 June 1960. This was a day after the official closure date of the line. *Derek Penney*

Right:
Just after Dingwall is the junction for the line to Kyle of Lochalsh. Dingwall had goods sidings, a locomotive shed and a spacious layout typical of so many Highland Railway stations. The cattle dock, complete with wagons, can be seen to the right of the approaching train — the 10.30am service from Inverness to Wick — with Type 2 No D5116 in charge on 9 August 1965. Note the TPO behind the locomotive in its rather striking scarlet livery. *Colour-Rail*

Left:
The BRCW Type 2 Bo-Bos dominated diesel haulage on the Highland lines, along with the BR Sulzer Type 2s, from the end of the 1950s until the mid-1970s when they were replaced by Class 37s. In the main locomotives have been replaced today by 'Sprinters' but, in 1966, the Type 2s were very much in charge and this photograph sees an unidentified member of the type on the Wick and Thurso mail from Inverness near Tain. Note again the TPO vehicle behind the locomotive.
Colour-Rail

Right:
Heading northwards, before Lairg, comes Bonar Bridge, complete with buffet, Culrain and, from there, the line crosses over the Kyle of Sutherland on a viaduct. Next is the small station at Invershin before Lairg is reached. On 21 June 1962 BR Type 2 (Class 24) No D5122 arrives at Lairg with a short freight. The locomotive carries the incorrect headcode '2' representing a local passenger service and not a freight train. Lairg had a small yard and passing loop. The Royal Mail ran a passenger bus from here to various communities. Bonar Bridge has subsequently been renamed Ardgay. *Colour-Rail*

Left:
Once past Rogart came The Mound, where the branch to Dornoch diverged. The Mound closed with the Dornoch branch on 13 June 1960, with goods services lingering on until 27 January 1964. The branch platforms were lower than those of the main line, a fact well illustrated in this photograph as ex-Highland Railway Drummond passenger tank No 55053 is seen shunting wagons that have arrived from the main line in May 1955. No 55053 is pictured in the Dornoch platform loop; the main line platforms can be seen to the right.
T. J. Edgington /Colour-Rail (SC350)

Above:
The immaculate station and yard at Dornoch is seen in 1955 with '0P' 0-4-4T No 55053 in charge of the usual mixed train, the 1pm for The Mound in June 1955. No 55053 was the last ex-Highland Railway locomotive to remain in BR service — preserved 'Jones Goods' No 103 doesn't count! — and was built at the HR's works at Lochgorm in Inverness in 1905. Unfortunately, a broken axle, sustained in 1957, on the leading pair of driving wheels was deemed to have put the locomotive beyond economic repair and it was withdrawn. The station building survives today as a take-away food outlet! *T. J. Edgington/Colour-Rail (SC134)*

Below:
The unlikely replacements for the ex-HR 0-4-4Ts were two ex-Great Western Railway (GWR) '16xx' 0-6-0PTs, Nos 1646 and 1649. The former is seen at Dornoch with the 1pm mixed service for The Mound in May 1957. This locomotive had the dubious honour of being the last steam locomotive to work on the Highland Railway system in regular service, being withdrawn in September 1962.
N. Sprinks/Colour-Rail (SC188)

Right:
From The Mound came the run up the coast through Golspie, the Duke of Sutherland's private station at Dunrobin, and then Brora where there was a loop and small yard. A Type 2 arrives at Brora with a service bound for Inverness in June 1966. The driver has just picked up the token and the train is crossing a northbound service. Note the large amount of mail on the platform waiting to be loaded .
A. E. Doyle/Colour-Rail

Left:

At Helmsdale there was a loop and once a turntable. The line's goal, Wick, is only 35 miles away as the crow flies, but there had to be an inland detour to avoid the high land of the Ord of Caithness which resulted in a route length of 60 miles. At Helmsdale a lovely scene sees the station and yard with Caledonian '3P' No 54495 on a short freight. A Highland TPO and a Gresley Buffet Car are stored in one of the sidings and the North Sea can be seen in the background. The locomotive shed at Helmsdale was coded 60C and, in 1950, had '3P' 4-4-0s Nos 54480 and 54489, Drummond passenger 0-4-4Ts Nos 55051 and 55053 and '3F' 0-6-0 No 57587 allocated to it. However, by 1959, there were the two ex-GWR interlopers, Nos 1646

and 1649, as well as more traditional '3P' 4-4-0s Nos 54470, 54480 and 54495 and '3F' 0-6-0 No 57587. F. W. *Shuttleworth/Colour-Rail (SC840)*

Above:

From Helmsdale, the line heads inland once again through Kildonan and Kinbrace. A BR Type 2 arrives at Forsinard from where the summit of the line is reached at County March — at 708ft — before isolated Altnabreac is reached. The other significant summit is just east of Lairg at 488ft. *Roy Hamilton*

Below:
Following Scotscalder, Georgemas Junction — the most northerly junction in Britain — is reached. Here trains to and from Wick and Thurso would split, although in some cases there was just a connection for Thurso. 'Jones Goods' No 103 is inevitably the centre of attraction as the locomotive runs round its train at the station during the joint RCTS/SLS tour of 15 June 1962. *Colour-Rail*

Right:
Type 2 D5128 (later No 24128) is seen at Georgemas Junction with the 06.15 service from Inverness to Wick on 30 March 1970. The train has stopped short and the two passenger coaches for Wick are left in front of the cabin, while the Thurso portion was shunted on to the Thurso engine standing on the branch. The train engine returned with the Wick BG, attached the Wick passenger coaches and is now pulling into the station prior to departing towards its ultimate destination.
Roy Hamilton

49

Above:
Wick was similar in design to Thurso, with a goods yard that was important for fish traffic, coal and general merchandise. Wick also had a locomotive shed (coded 60D). The station was also the terminus of the 13.75-mile-long light railway to Lybster. This light railway, where the rails were spiked directly onto the sleepers, opened on 1 July 1903 and closed completely as early as 1 April 1944. Preserved 'Jones Goods' No 103 is seen at Wick on 15 August 1962. The sidings either side of the station are full of vans — primarily for fish traffic. *Colour-Rail*

Right:
BRCW Type 2 (later Class 26) diesel-electrics Nos D5336/39 wait at Wick with the Wick portion of the 5pm service to Inverness on 4 July 1962. Parcels and goods are being loaded into the leading coach and the train would be combined with the Thurso portion at Georgemas Junction. *C. Woodhead/Colour-Rail*

51

Below:
The small two-road shed at Wick is seen with ex-Caledonian Railway Class 72 4-4-0 No 54495 outside. The locomotive is coded as 60C (Helmsdale) and Wick itself was coded as 60D. These Caledonian '3Ps' were common on the line as the older Highland types were withdrawn, having been displaced in their traditional areas by diesels and DMUs. In 1950 the allocation included a number of ex-HR designs. These were Nos 54398 *Ben Alder*, 54399 *Ben Wyvis* and 54404 *Ben Clebrig* as well as ex-CR '3P' No 54445 and ex-CR '3F' No 57585. In 1959 just three locomotives were allocated to Wick: Nos 40150, 54491 and 57585. The shed closed in 1962. *L. F. Folkhard/Colour-Rail*

Right:
Thurso is the most northerly station in Britain but there was also a small halt at Hoy between Thurso and Georgemas Junction. Thurso was also the nearest station to the Scapa Flow naval base (located in the Orkney Islands) and was busy with military personnel in both world wars. This was yet another example of the strategic importance of the ex-HR routes. Thurso also had sidings and an overall train shed. The latter can be seen to good effect here, as can Stanier-designed 2-6-4T No 40150 of 60D (Wick), which has just arrived on a service from Georgemas Junction on 28 August 1959. There was also a small locomotive shed at Thurso, which was a sub-shed of Wick. *Colour-Rail*

Above:
A view on 25 May 1974 sees the new order at Thurso as BR corporate blue, along with blue/grey carriages, predominates. A Class 24, No 24128, awaits departure for Georgemas Junction. Some of the goods sidings can also be seen. These were located either side of the station, but are less busy than in the 1950s and early 1960s.
Colour-Rail

Right:
From Dingwall began the 63-mile journey to Kyle of Lochalsh. The short branch to Strathpeffer, opened on 3 June 1865 and closed to passengers on 23 February 1946 and to freight on 12 August 1951, branched off at Fodderty Junction. The first station heading westwards after Fodderty Junction (where there was no station) was at Achterneed. This was closely followed by Garve, where Type 2 (later Class 24) No D5130 enters with the 10.30am service from Inverness to Kyle of Lochalsh on 21 May 1970. The train is formed of both passenger coaches and vans. Garve was the proposed junction in 1893 for a route heading northwestwards to serve Ullapool.
Roy Hamilton

Left:
Also pictured at Garve is the preserved 'Jones Goods' at the head of a mixed train on 21 May 1960. The first three vehicles in the consist are livestock wagons; it is easy to forget how important livestock traffic was to the railways until the early 1960s, as evidenced by the number of cattle docks at rural stations. Many farmers would argue that rail was a much better — and less stressful for the animals — means of moving livestock than today's road equivalent. *Colour-Rail*

Right:
The summer 1964 timetable or the Far North services from Inverness to Kyle of Lochlash, Wick and Thurso. *Peter Waller Collection*

Below:
Achnasheen was a crossing place and from here there was a bus that served Gairloch to the northwest. This bus also carried mail. There were proposals in 1892, which ultimately came to nothing, for a line running from a junction at Achnasheen that would have served Gairloch en route to Aultbea. This was one of a number of proposed routes serving remote parts of the Scottish Highlands that failed to materialise. 'Black 5' No 45361 is pictured with a rake of carmine and cream-liveried coaches calling at Achnasheen with a service for Inverness in 1956.
J. M. Jarvis/Colour-Rail

INVERNESS, KYLE OF LOCHALSH, THURSO and WICK

Miles from Inverness	Week Days only																	
		TC Glasgow to Thurso except Sunday nights and Monday mornings; TC Inverness to Wick and Thurso; RC Inverness to Kildonan	THE ORCADIAN Commences 26th June; TC Inverness to Wick	Commences 27th June MB Observation Car		TC Inverness to Wick and Thurso	RB Inverness to Wick	MB Observation Car until 26th June RC Inverness to Achnasheen			TC Inverness to Wick and Thurso							
		pm	am	am			am	am			am		am					
32	Glasgow (Buchanan St.) dep	11Z15	..	..	..		4L 0	4L 0	..	..	9 30	..	9 30	..	..	..	..	..
27	Edinburgh (Waverley) .. "	10N55	..	..	..		..	..	..	..	9B18	..	9B18	..	..	..	..	..
35	Perth .. "	1a25	..	..	..		6 55	6 55	..	..	11C12	..	11C12	..	..	..	..	..
		am	am	am			am	am			pm		pm					
—	**Inverness** dep	**6 40**	**9 5**	**9 25**	..		**10 30**	**10 40**	..	..	**4 55**	..	**5 40**	..	..	..	..	..
18¾	**Dingwall** arr	**7 8**	**9 32**	**9 55**	..		**10 58**	**11 9**	..	..	**5 25**	..	**6 9**	..	..	..	..	..
—	**Dingwall** dep	**7 13**	**9 33**	**9 58**	..		**11 1**	**11 19**	..	..	**5 26**	..	**6 14**	..	..	..	..	..
23½	Achterneed	..		10U 7	..		..	11 29	..	..	..	..	6 24	..	..	..	..	..
30½	Garve	..		10 23	..		..	11 45	..	..	..	..	6 40	..	..	..	..	..
35¾	Lochluichart	..		..	..		..	11 54	..	..	..	..	6 49	..	..	..	..	..
40¼	Achanalt	..		..	..		..	12p 7	..	..		..	7 7	..	..	..	..	..
46¼	Achnasheen	..		10 57	..			12 21	..	..		..	7 21	..	..	..	..	..
55	Glencarron	..		..	..			12P36	..	..		..	7P36	..	..	..	..	..
59	Achnashellach	..		..	..			12 45	..	..		..	7 45	..	..	..	..	..
64½	Strathcarron	..		11 38	..			12 56	..	..		..	7 56	..	..	..	..	..
66¾	Attadale	..		..	..			1 0	..	..		..	8 0	..	..	..	..	..
72	Stromeferry	..		11S54	..			1 14	..	..		..	8 14	..	..	..	..	..
75¾	Duncraig	..		..	..			1 22	..	..		..	8N22	..	..	..	..	..
77	Plockton	..		..	..			1 26	..	..		..	8 26	..	..	..	..	..
78¼	Duirinish	..		..	..			1 30	..	..		..	8 30	..	..	..	..	..
82¼	**Kyle of Lochalsh** arr	..		**12 20**	..			**1 40**	..	..		..	**8 40**	..	..	..	..	..
31¼	Invergordon dep	7 31	9 48		..		11 19		..	..	5 43	..	..	..	..	..	..	..
40½	Fearn	7 45	..		..		11 32		..	..	5 56	..	..	..	..	..	..	..
44	**Tain** arr	**7 53**	**10 5**		..		**11 40**		..	..	**6 3**	..	..	..	..	..	..	..
	dep	**7 55**	**10 6**		..		**11 41**		..	..	**6 4**	..	..	..	..	..	..	..
57½	Bonar Bridge	8 15	10 24		..		12p 3		..	..	6 23	..	..	..	..	..	..	..
60¾	Culrain	8 23	..		..		12 10		..	..	6 30	..	..	..	..	..	..	..
61	Invershin	8 26	..		..		12 13		..	..	6 33	..	..	..	..	..	..	..
66¾	Lairg	8 41	10 40		..		12 27		..	..	6 46	..	..	..	..	..	..	..
76¾	Rogart Halt	8 59	..		..		..		..	..	7 3	..	..	..	..	..	..	..
84	Golspie	9 10	11 4		..		12 51		..	..	7 15	..	..	..	..	..	..	..
86	Dunrobin (Private)	9P14	..		..		1P55		..	..	7P20	..	..	..	..	..	..	..
90¼	Brora	9 23	11 15		..		1 3		..	..	7 28	..	..	..	..	..	..	..
101¼	**Helmsdale** arr	**9 40**	**11 32**		..		**1 20**		..	..	**7 45**	..	..	..	..	..	..	..
	dep	**9 44**	**11 35**		..		**1 28**		..	..	**7 46**	..	..	..	..	..	..	..
104	Salzcraggie	9P48			..		..		..	..	..	..	..	..	..	..	..	..
110¾	Kildonan	10 5			..		1 42		..	..	7N59	..	..	..	..	..	..	..
114½	Borrobol	10N13		..	..		..		..	..	8P 5	..	..	..	..	..	..	..
113	Kinbrace	10 22		..	..		1 55		..	..	8N11	..	..	..	..	..	..	..
125½	Forsinard	10 35		..	..		2 11		..	..	8N23	..	..	..	..	..	..	..
133¾	Altnabreac	10 49		..	..		2 28		..	..	8N36	..	..	..	..	..	..	..
142¾	Scotscalder	11 4		..	..		2 43		..	..	8N50	..	..	..	..	..	..	..
147	**Georgemas Junction** arr	**11 12**	**12p41**	..	..		**2 51**		..	..	**8 57**	..	..	..	..	..	..	..
—	**Georgemas Junction** dep	**11 22**	**12 43**	..	..		**2 56**	..	..	..	**9 5**	..	..	..	..	..	..	..
151	Hoy	11P21	..	..	..		3P 2	..	..	..	..	..	..	..	..	..	..	..
153¾	**Thurso** arr	**11 35**	**1 5**	..	..		**3 15**	..	..	..	**9 22**	..	..	..	..	..	..	..
161¼	**Wick** arr	**11 40**	**1 5**	..	..		**3 15**	..	..	..	**9 23**	..	..	..	..	..	..	..

a am
B On Saturdays only from 27th June to 29th August inclusive depart 10 3 am
C Except Saturdays depart 11 12 am. On Saturdays 20th June and 5th September depart 11 15 am and on Saturdays from 27th June to 29th August inclusive depart 11 49 am
H Except Saturday and Sunday nights

L Departs from Glasgow (Central) Station
MB Miniature Buffet Car
N Stops to take up and set down on notice at previous station
P Stops to take up when passengers on platform and on notice at previous stopping station to set down
p pm

RB Buffet Car
RC Restaurant Car
S Saturdays only
TC Through Carriages
U Stops on notice to take up
Z Depart Glasgow (Buchanan Street) 11 15 pm, except Saturdays and 11 25 pm on Sundays

Left:
Glencarron Platform was added to the line in 1873, after it had opened, along with Lochluichart and Achnashellach, which had both opened in 1871. 'Black 5' No 44978 provided the motive power for a railtour organised by the RCTS and SLS. The special is pictured at Glencarron on 14 June 1962. *Colour-Rail*

Right:
Achnashellach is seen on 21 May 1960 with the preserved 'Jones Goods' No 103 on a mixed parcels and freight. The station at Achnashellach opened in 1871. *Colour Rail*

Left:

BRCW Type 2 — now reclassified Class 26 and renumbered — No 26046 heads an Inverness train at Strome Ferry in July 1974. This was the original terminus of the line, where passengers boarded a ship for Kyle and the Isle of Skye before the opening of the extension to Kyle of Lochalsh. Strome Ferry was later the site of the Howard Doris sidings that were built to supply the construction site at Loch Kishorn for the Ninian oil field. These sidings saw trains of fly ash, cement and building materials come to the line. Indeed, such was the level of this traffic (which was predicted to increase), that it was sufficient to see the line reprieved — it had been under threat of closure from 1973. However, the traffic did not flourish and the sidings closed in September 1977. *Colour-Rail*

Right:

A BR Type 2 heads a very mixed — but common on the line — train from Kyle to Inverness at Duirinish in February 1974. Duirinish is the last station on the section of line from Strome Ferry to Kyle of Lochalsh before the terminus is reached. *Colour-Rail*

Left:
Preserved 'Jones Goods' No 103 heads a mixed train away from Kyle of Lochalsh on the journey to Dingwall and Inverness in 1959. It is seen passing Erbusaig — just north of Kyle — and the spectacular scenery the line passes through is well illustrated before arrival at Kyle, which was accessed by blasting through a rock cutting. Originally, due to the cost of constructing this section, trains terminated at Strome Ferry where passengers and freight had to travel to Kyle and Skye by ship. *The late Derek Cross/Colour-Rail*

Right:
The locomotive shed at Kyle of Lochalsh was coded 60A and was a sub-shed of Inverness. 'Black 5' No 45192 and two companions are seen on the shed in 1956. *B. J. Swain/Colour-Rail*

Left:
Kyle of Lochalsh station replaced the earlier terminus at Strome Ferry in the 1890s and was built by blasting a way to the station area through the local granite. This allowed the railway to connect with the ferry to the Isle of Skye, which can be seen in the background, and steamers to Stornoway. In addition to the pier, there was a large goods yard for traffic to and from the Western Isles and for fish. David MacBrayne's steamers took over from those originally run by the Highland Railway. Apart from the changes to locomotives and rolling stock, the scene at Kyle on 25 August 1965 is remarkably similar to former years as No D5341 is seen on an Inverness train, complete with the 'Devon Belle' observation car, which was transferred north from the Southern Region to provide passengers with enhanced views. *J. M. Boyes/Colour-Rail*

Right:
'Black 5' No 44978, working the RCTS/SLS Scottish Railtour and seen earlier on the Kyle line at Glencarron, has now reached Nairn on 16 June 1962. Nairn had two signalboxes and is located 15 miles from Inverness. The Inverness & Nairn Railway was the first part of the future Highland Railway to be opened, this occurring on 5 November 1855. *Colour-Rail*

Left:
The next station east from Nairn on the line towards Forres was Auldearn. Two ex-CR Class 3P 4-4-0s, Nos 54485 and 54486, head towards Forres with the 2.5pm service from Inverness to Aviemore on 21 May 1960. From Forres, the train will take the original HR main line south through Grantown-on-Spey West and Boat of Garten to Aviemore. *Colour-Rail*

Right:
Forres station was located on a triangle. This arrangement allowed a connection to the original main line to Aviemore from either the Inverness or Elgin direction. Before the opening of the line to the south it was a normal two-platform affair. Type 2 (later Class 26) No D5332 is seen at Forres on the west to south curve platform with the 9.40am service from Inverness to Glasgow Buchanan Street via Dava on 16 June 1962. A train for Inverness can be seen on the main west to east line in the background. *Roy Hamilton*

Above:
'Black 5' No 44978 is seen at Forres on the RCTS/SLS Scottish Railtour. The locomotive is standing on the main eastbound through line from Inverness to Aberdeen on 16 June 1962. The goods yard can be seen to the right. There was also a goods loop through here which was, in fact, the original main line complete with the original passenger station. *Roy Hamilton*

Right:
The locomotive shed at Forres, coded 60E, was a small two-road structure and was located directly behind the photographer in this view taken on 8 June 1957. Looking westwards, two ex-Caledonian locomotives can be seen: on the left is Class 3P 4-4-0 No 54473 and on the right Class 2P 0-4-4T No 55178. Forres shed was to close in 1959 and, just prior to its closure, the shed was home to six locomotives: '3Ps' Nos 54471/72/73, '2P' 0-4-4T No 55269, '3F' 0-6-0T No 56291 and '3F' 0-6-0 No 57620. *Colour-Rail*

Left:
On 14 June 1960, during the joint SLS/RCTS
Scottish Railtour of that year, Class 2P 4-4-0
No 40663 awaits departure from Elgin. In the
background a Standard Class 2 2-6-0 waits with a
normal service. Elgin was the scene of much dispute
between the GNoSR and the Highland. It had a
substantial network with lines to Lossiemouth,
Buckie, a line south to Craigellachie and Keith, as
well as the direct Highland main line from Inverness
to Aberdeen. The GNoSR also constructed a line
from Keith to Elgin via the coast through Fortessie
and Buckie. Disputes occurred over the exchange of
traffic and in the end the GNoSR applied to build its
own line to Inverness but this failed and thus it
applied for running powers to Inverness over the
Highland. In the end, an agreement was reached that
Elgin should be the exchange point between the HR
and the GNoSR, thus keeping the latter out of
Inverness. *Frank Hornby/Colour-Rail*

Right:
'Black 5' No 45476 leaves Elgin on 14 June 1960.
In the background the '2P' No 40663 waits for her
special train duty. The train is coming on to the
Inverness main line, seen immediately in the
foreground, off the ex-GNoSR line that branched to
Lossiemouth. To the north of the station, shortly
along the branch to Lossiemouth, a further junction
saw a second ex-GNoSR line head south towards
Craigellachie and thence to Keith Junction,
providing an alternative route to the ex-HR line
between Keith and Elgin. This line was originally
part of the Morayshire Railway, and before it was
built, access to Craigellachie was via a short spur
from Orton on the Elgin to Keith line to Rothes.
However, this was closed as early as 1866 when the
through line via Coleburn took most of its traffic.
Derek Penney

Left:
The Aberdeen-Inverness service was operated by the magnificent Swindon-built DMUs for many years until they were replaced by Class 37s and then by 'Sprinters'. The 11.45 from Aberdeen to Inverness calls at the Highland station at Elgin on 8 April 1967. *Roy Hamilton*

Below:
Class 2P No 40663 is seen at Burghead on the SLS/RCTS Scottish Railtour on 14 June 1960. The branch to Burghead originally operated as far as Hopeman, but the section beyond Burghead was closed to passengers on 14 September 1931, with freight ceasing on 31 December 1957. The section from Burghead to Alves, on the main line, was also closed to passengers on 14 September 1931 but is still open today for freight traffic as far as Roseisle. The '2P' was a post-Grouping LMS development of a Midland design and weighed just over 54 tons. No 40663 was a Kittybrewster-allocated locomotive at this time. Note the Camping Coach in the horse dock behind the train. *Roy Hamilton*

Below:
Keith shed (61C) is seen in August 1954 and yields a treasure trove of locomotives. These are 'B12/4' No 61539 (a visitor from Kittybrewster), 'D40' No 62264 (which was based at Keith) and, from Forres, '3P' No 54482. A 'K2' and another 'D40' are also seen. Keith Junction was the Highland station from where the GNoSR line branched off to serve Keith Town and then Craigellachie to access Elgin via the GNoSR line and Aviemore via Grantown-on-Spey East. The shed was actually ex-GNoSR. The main line to Keith Junction passes by to the left of the photographer. *E. S. Russell/Colour-Rail (SC189)*

Right:
Heading south from Forres on the original main line to Aviemore, the first station to be encountered was that at Dunphail (although there was another station, Rafford, that only lasted from 1863 until 1865). Pictured at Dunphail Viaduct on 21 May 1960 are two ex-CR 4-4-0s, Nos 54485/86, heading the 2.5pm service from Inverness southwards towards Aviemore and Perth. The two veterans had operated northbound the previous day when their trip from Perth to Aviemore had been recorded by Patrick Whitehouse and John Adams as one of the features in the TV series *Railway Roundabout*. No 54486 was the last of the batch to be built, emerging from the CR works at St Rollox in 1920; it was to remain in service until March 1962, outliving No 54485 by a few months. *Eric Russell/Colour-Rail*

Forres-Aviemore (via Dava)

Left:
The joint SLS/RCTS Scottish Railtour is seen near the summit at Dava behind 'Black 5' No 44978 on 16 June 1962. There was also a station at Dava and the line continued on the descent to Aviemore through Grantown-on-Spey and Broomhill. It also passed through Boat of Garten where the line met the GNoSR route from Craigellachie and Keith.
Colour Rail

Right:
From 'the Boat' the line continued to Aviemore, where one of the Park Royal-built four-wheel railbuses, No 79973, is pictured in the sidings awaiting its next duty on the Craigellachie via Boat of Garten service. It was hoped that these small units would be the saviour of some of the rural branch lines. However, the real problem was actually the number of other operational staff. Possibly with radio signalling and other initiatives more of these lines would still be open today.
A. G. Forsyth/Colour-Rail (DE1630)

Endpiece

Left:
With Keith Town station and the GNoSR line to Craigellachie now closed (although still extant as far as Dufftown) and now the subject of a preservation scheme, class 158 No 158705 represents the new order at Keith (formerly Keith Junction) – the highland station on 16 July 1996, with the 11.35 service from Aberdeen to Inverness. *Roy Hamilton*

Above:
There can be no more fitting way of concluding this survey of the former Highland Railway in the late 1950s and early 1960s, than to portray the only surviving ex-HR locomotive — the 'Jones Goods' 4-6-0 No 103 — amidst the superb scenery for which the Highlands of Scotland are rightly famed — a truly splendid sight. The locomotive is hauling an eastbound service from Kyle of Lochalsh to Inverness along the southern shore of Loch Carron. *John Adams/Colour-Rail*

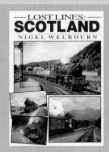
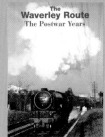
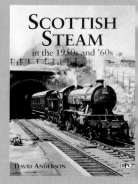

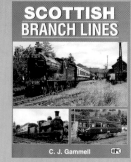